Comfort in Sorrow

Dedicated to the memory of my parents

I know that our nature asks and seeks for its friends and daily companions; it cannot but be grieved. So weep at the death of a dear one, not as disbelieving the Resurrection, but as not enduring the separation; for you are bidding farewell to one setting out on a journey for distant lands.

St John Chrysostom: Homily 62 on St John

With grateful acknowledgements of the assistance of Gerard Tracey, Archivist of the Birmingham Oratory.

Comfort in Sorrow

John Henry Newman

Words in Time of Bereavement

edited by James Tolhurst

First published in 1996

Gracewing
Fowler Wright Books
2 Southern Ave, Leominster
Herefordshire HR6 0QF

ISBN 0 85244 306 4

Typesetting by Action Typesetting Ltd,
Gloucester, GL1 1SP

Printed by Redwood Books,
Trowbridge, Wiltshire, BA14 8RN

Contents

Preface

John Henry Newman (1801–1890) is known best as the great preacher and the composer of incomparable prose. Biographers concentrate on aspects of his character which justify his position in the annals of the nineteenth century. Few, however, are concerned with his impact on the circle of his friends and relations, because this does not make history.

But what differentiates Newman from many of his contemporaries was his great humanity. There are those who have done greater things in their lives, and written more enduring literary works, but few have been more deeply loved. Those who examine Newman's life as a series of achievements – and failures – miss the constant thread of that daily contact with those among whom he lived and worked. He was truly interested in them as a friend who cared and loved them and nowhere is this more clearly brought out than when they suffered bereavements.

Death was a frequent visitor to Victorian households. Before 1900 over fifteen per cent of children died before adolescence. Isaac Williams could preface his memoirs to his family, truthfully '… If any of you should live to manhood'. People before the war were accustomed to witness death close at hand, in their own home. This is increasingly rare today. As a result, our own outlook has undergone a change because the fact of death has become that much more remote and this has coincided with the rise of doubts about immortality itself.

On the one hand is that agnosticism in the face of death which talks in terms of

The vast moth-eaten musical brocade
Created to pretend we never die

of Philip Larkin. On the other is that well of sentimentality which lies ever ready to spill over, tapped into so profitably by Charles Dickens. In our present situation we are unhappy with agnosticism and not quite at home with sentimentality, but we are still faced with the fact of bereavement.

When we read Newman dealing with the death of those he had known and loved we discover a different approach. As a young man he had been witness to a particularly tragic death – that of a favourite sister, Mary, apparently of a heart condition. His father had died four years previously and he would bury his mother from Littlemore in 1836. As a curate he was almost every day at the bed-side of dying parishioners many of whom he meticulously recorded later in his book of anniversaries. But whereas death tends to embitter many, for Newman it formed part of that realisation of the presence of God which must lie at the root of all friendships: 'If we enjoy the presence of friends, let them remind us of the Communion of Saints before His throne'. Those whom we love are lost to us for a while, but still love us in the presence of God to whom they go. In a sense they are closer to us when they have left this earthly life: 'For those we love are not nearest to us when in the flesh, but they come into our very hearts as being spiritual beings, when they are removed from us'.

It was this conviction which underlay Newman's sympathy to those who were bereaved. He reminded them of the reality of the next life and our communion with the faithful departed. He is only reiterating what Cassian wrote so many years ago 'He can be sure that in eternity he will have as his lot the service and companionship which he preferred in this life'. But at the same time he enters into the suffering of those to whom he preaches and writes: 'True compassion is that union between our souls and the suffering object of our love.'

It is that mixture which was found so helpful, as we know, for instance in the reply which Henry Edward Manning wrote to Newman just after the death of his wife: 'I hardly know what has drawn me so closely, and in one way suddenly to your sympathy, but I feel something in the way you deal with my sorrows, particularly soothing and strengthening'. He teaches us that reverence for death which accompanies those who are bereaved with a friendship too deep for mere expressions: 'too personal to me for me to be able to say any words of comfort to you, except that sympathy is comfort'.

We can also be strengthened by Newman's own witness that 'God has never failed me. He has at all times been to me a faithful God.' He was consistent in his life right to the end and Fr Neville, his close friend and secretary tells us that forty eight hours before he died 'he entered his room a little before he was expected – his footstep was slow, yet firm and elastic; indeed it was not recognized as his; his attendant was surprised that it was he; soon, when seen, his bearing was in keeping with his step – unbent, erect to the full height of his best days in the fifties (the Cardinal was 89); he was without support of any kind. His whole carriage was, it may be said, soldier-like, and so dignified; and his countenance was most attractive to look at; even old age seemed to have gone from his face; and with it all care-worn signs; his very look conveyed the cheerfulness and gratitude of his mind, and what he said was so kind; his voice was quite fresh and strong; his whole appearance was that of power combined with complete calm – and it might be said – with readiness to die.' We need to express that confidence in God into whose presence we should *long* to go when this life is over, which will soften all anguish and bring to mind what we may have lost sight of while we go forth about our work until we reach the evening, for 'both young and old go "as little children" into the presence of their God'.

James Tolhurst
Edgbaston

And so again, to take a different case, many men, when they come near persons in distress and wish to show sympathy, often condole in a very unreal way. I am not altogether laying this to their fault; for it is very difficult to know what to do, when on the one hand we cannot realize to ourselves the sorrow, yet withal wish to be kind to those who feel it. A tone of grief seems necessary, yet (if so be) cannot under our circumstances be genuine. Yet even here surely there is a true way, if we could find it, by which pretence may be avoided, and yet respect and consideration shown.

Family Bereavements

A Blessed and Ever Enduring Fellowship

Newman recalls in his diary on 5 January, 1828 'We lost my sister Mary suddenly'

And now how can I summon the strength to recount the particulars of the heaviest affliction with which the good hand of God has ever visited me? ... Here every thing reminds me of her. She was with us at Oxford, and I took a delight in showing her the place – and every building, every tree, seems to speak of her. I cannot realize that I shall never see her again.

We are not separated from those who have died ...

Can the tyranny of earth hinder our holding a blessed and ever-enduring fellowship with those who are dead, by consulting their wishes, and dwelling upon their image, and trying to imitate them, and imagining their peaceful state, and sympathizing in their 'loud cry'[1] and hoping to meet them hereafter? No, truly! ... They are present still! We are not solitary, though we seem so. Few now alive may understand or sanction us; but those multitudes in the primitive time, who believed, and taught, and worshipped, as we do, still live unto God, and, in their past deeds and their present voices, cry from the Altar. They animate us by their example; they cheer us by their company; they are on our right hand and our left, Martyrs, Confessors, and the like, high and low, who used the same Creeds, and celebrated the same Mysteries, and preached the same Gospel as we do.

[1] Heb 5, 7

The friendship with Frederic Rogers began when Newman coached him through his finals. He had written to Newman to tell him that his sister was dying

1 June, 1837

Your letter of this morning made me very sad indeed. It was exceedingly kind in you to say what you have, and I feel it very much. Ever since I asked you what I did so abruptly, when you were here, not knowing how matters stood, I have borne your sister continually in mind, and was anxious to hear how things were. I am certain you do not anticipate what is still future *hastily*, but I know I should just do the same in your case. If it is to turn out as you forebode, it is only a fresh instance of what I suppose one must make up one's mind to think, and what is consoling to think, that those who are early taken away are the fittest to be taken, and that it is a privilege so to be taken, and they are in their proper place when taken. Surely God would not separate from us such, except it were best both for them and for us, and that those who are taken away are such as are most acceptable to Him seems proved by what we see; for scarcely do you hear of some especial instance of religious excellence, but you have also cause of apprehension how long such a one is to continue here. I suppose one ought to take it as the rule. We pray daily 'Thy kingdom come' – if we understand our words, we mean it as a privilege to leave the world, and we must not wonder that God grants the privilege to some of those who pray for it. It would be rather wonderful if He did not.

5

Christ will acknowledge his image in us

Let us never lose sight of this great and simple view, which the whole of Scripture sets before us. What was actually done by Christ in the flesh eighteen hundred years ago, is in type and resemblance really wrought in us one by one even to the end of time. He was born of the Spirit, and we too are born of the Spirit. He was justified by the Spirit, and so are we ... He offered Himself to death by the Eternal Spirit; He was raised from the dead by the Spirit; He was declared to be the Son of God by the Spirit of holiness on His resurrection: we too are led by the same Spirit into and through this world's temptation; we, too, do our works of obedience by the Spirit; we die from sin, we rise again unto righteousness through the Spirit; and we are declared to be God's sons, – declared, pronounced, dealt with as righteous, – through our resurrection unto holiness in the Spirit ... We are ever receiving our birth, our justification, our renewal, ever dying to sin, ever rising to righteousness. His whole economy in all its parts is ever in us all at once; and this divine presence constitutes the title of each of us to heaven; this is what He will acknowledge and accept at the last day. He will acknowledge Himself, – His image in us, – as though we reflected Him, and He, on looking round about discerned at once who were His; those, namely, who gave back to Him His image. He impresses us with the seal of the Spirit, in order to avouch that we are His. As the king's image appropriates the coin to him, so the likeness of Christ in us separates us from the world and assigns us over to the kingdom of heaven.

*Eliza Froude, known as Isy, the eldest daughter of
William Froude had informed Newman that her
grandfather, Arthur Howe Holdsworth, Governor of
Dartmouth Castle had just died*

16 May, 1860

My dear Child,

Thank you for your letter of yesterday – Today's post
brings an account of your Grandfather's death. It must be
an extreme trial to your mother and aunt – but God orders
all things, and we must recollect that He is infinitely more
tender and kind and merciful to every one of us, than we
can be, and that, in going to Him, we are going to One who
knows of what we are made, and, as knowing us, is able to
be indulgent in a way in which *we* cannot be to those even
whom we know best.

Mama most kindly wrote me some days ago, asking after
my health. I will not intrude upon her with my answer at
this moment, but I will tell her through you, and you can
tell her when you think it best.

Tell her then, that I never was in better health or in more
perfect activity of mind. On the other hand I cannot deny
that all last year I was getting more and more an old man,
and that I am still going on in the same process – that my
hair is getting whiter and whiter, and my fingers thinner and
thinner, and that I cannot get rid of my hoarseness quite.

But tell her, that, please God, I shall not love her and all
of you less and less, or lose my affectionate interest in all
that concerns you, or forget to pray for you, though I
dwindle and fade away into a spider's web.

We will rise from our sorrow ...

One more remark I shall make, and then conclude. It must not be supposed, because the doctrine of the Cross makes us sad, that therefore the Gospel is a sad religion. The Psalmist says, 'They that sow in tears shall reap in joy;' and our Lord says, 'They that mourn shall be comforted.' Let no one go away with the impression that the Gospel makes us take a gloomy view of the world and of life. It hinders us indeed from taking a superficial view, and finding a vain transitory joy in what we see; but it forbids our immediate enjoyment, only to grant enjoyment in truth and fulness afterwards. It only forbids us to *begin* with enjoyment. It only says, If you begin with pleasure, you will end with pain. It bids us begin with the Cross of Christ, and in that Cross we shall at first find sorrow, but in a while peace and comfort will rise out of that sorrow. That Cross will lead us to mourning, repentance, humiliation, prayer, fasting; we shall sorrow for our sins, we shall sorrow with Christ's sufferings; but all this sorrow will only issue, nay, will be undergone in a happiness far greater than the enjoyment which the world gives, – though careless worldly minds indeed will not believe this, ridicule the notion of it, because they never have tasted it, and consider it a mere matter of words, which religious persons think it decent and proper to use, and try to believe themselves, and to get others to believe, but which no one really feels. This is what they think; but our Saviour said to His disciples, 'Ye now therefore have sorrow, but I will see you again, and your heart shall rejoice, and your joy no man taketh from you.' ... 'Peace I leave with you; My peace I give unto you; not as the world giveth, give I unto you.' And St. Paul says, 'The

8

natural man receiveth not the things of the Spirit of God; for they are foolishness unto him; neither can he know them, because they are spiritually discerned.' 'Eye hath not seen, nor ear heard, neither have entered into the heart of man, the things which God hath prepared for them that love Him.'[1]

[1] John 16, 22. 14, 27; 1 Cor 2, 9.14

Henry Bowden's second wife, Marianne Burgoyne died on 26 June. Newman had married them at St George's Hanover Square in 1838. Six daughters and a son were orphaned

28 June, 1864

My dear Children,

You have all begun life with one of the greatest trials you can have till the end of it. You can but lose a Mother once. God support you under it – and I know He will. Take a delight in kissing His rod, when He strikes you – as if you saw it – and the taste of it will be sweet to your lips. The Almighty Paraclete will be with you, and give you great consolation amid your great grief.

We have been saying Mass for the Soul of dear Mama this morning. I have been saying Mass for her daily – yesterday 'as alive or departed'. Fr Neville has said a great many Masses too, and Fr St. John. I think of each of you, my dear girls, separately, and of dear Willie. I know what a thoughtful boy he is – he looks calm and quiet, but he has many thoughts – and, though he is little, he will learn to be a support to his sisters. And you will all of you be a support to each other – every one to all the rest – And now the worst is over – that is the great thing. It is indeed most piercing to see the pain of those we love and not to be able to help them – a wall of separation between oneself and them! But it is all over – and don't doubt that all the suffering which she has had, borne so bravely and lovingly, has brought her near to God, and to a state of peace and rest. And now, while you bid adieu for a while, only for a while, to dearest Mama, offer yourselves, my dear children, to your great and tender Mother in heaven, the Blessed Mother of God, who will not refuse to have you, and to watch over you, and to give you all that gentle and true guidance which you need so much, and which you hoped to have from her whom God has taken from you. But all He does is good, and we shall see and know it one day – Let us trust in Him meanwhile, and pray Him, that, when our turn comes, we may die as happily and hopefully, as she has died for whom we mourn.

Cf. p. 33

And Jesus wept

When, then, our Saviour weeps from sympathy at Mary's tears, let us not say it is the love of a man overcome by natural feeling. It is the love of God ... Jesus wept, therefore, not merely from the deep thoughts of His understanding but from spontaneous tenderness; from the gentleness and mercy, the encompassing loving-kindness and exuberant fostering affection of the Son of God for His own work, the race of man. Their tears touched Him at once, as their miseries had brought Him down from heaven. His ear was open to them, and the sound of weeping went at once to His heart.

James Robert Hope-Scott was a legal adviser and confidant. He had died after a long and painful illness on 29 April. Newman wrote to his daughter Mary

30 April, 1873

My dear Child

You alone can know what it is to be bereaved of such a Father. You never can have a heavier blow, because you are so young and so untried in suffering. But God is more than enough to make up all to you, and He will. You will look back with tender affection, not only on happy past days, but on this long sad time, when hope rose and fell again, and you felt weary of the changes.

May you be as great a blessing to all around you, as he has been.

For me, his departure is a memento that my day must come. May I be as prepared as he.

*Newman preached his panegyric at Farm Street on
5 May, 1873 on the text of 1 John 2,17*

I only know what he was to me. I only know what his loss
is to me. I only know that he is one of those whose departure hence has made the heavens dark to me. But I have
never lived with him, or travelled with him; I have seen him
from time to time; I have visited him; I have corresponded
with him; I have had mutual confidences with him. Our
lines of duty have lain in very different directions. I have
known him as a friend knows friend in the tumult and
hurry of life. I have known him well enough to know how
much more there was to know in him; and to look forward,
alas! in vain, to a time when, in the evening and towards the
close of life, I might know him more. I have known him
enough to love him very much, and to sorrow very much,
that here I shall not see him again. But then I reflect, if I,
who do not know him as he might be known, suffer as I
do, what must be their suffering who knew him so well?

...

But those for whom God has a love more than ordinary
He watches over with no ordinary jealousy; and, if the
world smiles on them, He sends them crosses and penances
so much the more. He is not content that they should be
by any common title His; and, because they are so dear to
Him, He provides for them afflictions to bring them nearer
still. I hope it is not presumptuous thus to speak of the
inscrutable providences of God. I know that He has His
own wise and special dealings with each one of us, and that
what He determines for one is no rule for another. I am
contemplating, and, if so be, interpreting, His loving ways
and purposes only towards the very man before us ... I may

14

speak with more vivid knowledge of him here than in other respects, for I was one of the confidants of his extreme suffering under the succession of terrible inflictions, which left wounds never to be healed. They ended only with his life; for the complaint, which eventually mastered him, was brought into activity by his final bereavement. Nay, I must not consider even that great bereavement his final one; his call to go hence was itself the final agony of that tender, loving heart. He who had in time past been left desolate by others, was now to leave others desolate. He was to be torn away, as if before his time, from those who, to speak humanly, needed him so exceedingly. He was called upon to surrender them in faith to Him who had given them. It was about two hours before his death, with this great sacrifice, as we may suppose, this solemn summons of his Supreme Lord confronting him, that he said, with a loud voice, 'Thy will be done'.

They were almost his last words.

Elizabeth Johnson had written to tell Newman that her mother, the widow of Manuel Johnson, the Radcliffe Observer, had died on 2 January

5 January, 1881

My dear Child

I hear with great sorrow of your and your Sister's loss – with personal sorrow, for your dear Mother was only one of a number, whom I began to know and to love about sixty years ago. I knew your Grandfather before his marriage, and, as his large family gradually formed and grew up, I knew them all. And, when he lost your Grandmother in 1835, it was I whom in the sad week that followed he let see his grief, and whose attempts to comfort him he accepted. And I have always kept all of you in mind, though I have been away from you.

But of course it is your own grief, my dear Children, which touches me most now. This is the last, and, being the last, the greatest of several great trials which have come upon you, and you need a great consolation. But God is good, and will be with you, I know; and there is no strength like that which He gives. He can make the heaviest trials light, 'When my Father and Mother forsake me,' it is said, 'He taketh me up.'[1] I said Mass for your dear Mother yesterday, and have entered her name in my Obituary,[2] and will not forget you all in the forlornness and heaviness which you are sure to undergo.

We too must say, after him, 'Thy will be done'. Let us be

[1] Ps 27, 10
[2] Newman's Obituary Book of anniversaries

16

sure that those whom God loves He takes away, each of them, one by one, at the very time best for their eternal interests. What can we, in sober earnest, wish, save that very will of God? Is He not wiser and more loving than we are? Could we wish him back whom we have lost? Who is there of us who loves him most but would feel the cruelty of recalling to this tumultuous life, with its spiritual perils and its dark future, a soul who is already rejoicing in the end and issue of his trial, in salvation secured, and heaven begun in him? Rather, who would not wish to have lived his life, and to have died his death? How well for him that he lived, not for man only, but for God! What are all the interests, pleasure, successes, glories of this world, when we come to die?

How different is the feeling with which the loving soul, on its separation from the body, approaches the judgment-seat of its Redeemer! It knows how great a debt of punishment remains upon it, though it has for many years been reconciled to him; it knows that purgatory lies before it, and that the best it can reasonably hope for is to be sent there. But to see His face, though for a moment! To hear His voice, to hear Him speak, though it be to punish! O Saviour of men, it says, I come to thee, though it be in order to be at once remanded from Thee; I come to Thee who art my Life and my All; I come to Thee on the thought of whom I have lived all my life long. To Thee I gave myself when first I had to take a part in the world; I sought Thee for my chief good early, for early didst thou teach me, that good elsewhere there was none. Whom have I in heaven but Thee? Whom have I desired on earth, whom have I had on earth, but Thee? Whom shall I have amid the sharp flame but Thee?

What we see is the outward shell of an eternal kingdom

The earth that we see does not satisfy us; it is but a beginning; it is but a promise of something beyond it; even when it is gayest, with all its blossoms on, and shows most touchingly what lies in it, yet it is not enough. We know much more lies hid in it than we see. A world of Saints and Angels, a glorious world, the palace of God, the mountain of the Lord of Hosts, the heavenly Jerusalem, the throne of God and Christ, all these wonders, everlasting, all-precious, mysterious, and incomprehensible, lie hid in what we see. What we see is the outward shell of an eternal kingdom; and on that kingdom we fix the eyes of our faith. Shine forth, O Lord, as when of Thy Nativity Thine Angels visited the shepherds; let Thy glory blossom forth as bloom and foliage on the trees; change with Thy mighty power this visible world into that diviner world, which as yet we see not; destroy what we see, that it may pass and be transformed into what we believe. Bright as is the sun, and the sky, and the clouds; green as are the leaves and the fields; sweet as is the singing of the birds; we know that they are not all, and we will not take up with a part for the whole. They proceed from a centre of love and goodness, which is God Himself; but they are not His fulness; they speak of heaven, but they are not heaven; they are but crumbs from the table.

The Hon. Mrs Maxwell-Scott had received the news that the husbands of two of her sisters had died within three weeks of each other

17 March, 1882

My dear Mamo,

You have indeed accumulated sorrow.

One's consolations under such trials, which are our necessary lot here, is that we have additional friends in heaven to plead and interest themselves for us. This I am confident of – if it is not presumptuous to be confident – but I think, as life goes on, it will be brought home to you, as it has been to me, that there are those who are busied about us, and in various daily matters taking our part.

Being Left Alone

The Loss of Husband or Wife

Pusey's wife, Maria was despaired of and died eight days later

18 May, 1839

My dear Pusey,

I hardly know how to answer your note, except that I will not forget what you say. But it seems to me you must not suffer yourself to suppose that any punishment is meant in what is now to be. Why should it? I mean, really it is nothing out of God's usual dealing. The young and strong fall all around us. How many whom we love are taken out of our sight by sudden death, however healthy – Whether slowly or suddenly, it comes on those in whose case we do not expect it. I do not think you must look on it as 'some strange thing.' Pray do not.

26 May, 1839

This, you will see, requires no answer. I have nothing to say – only I wish you to remember that many persons are thinking of you and making mention of you, where you wish to be mentioned. Do not fear you will not be strengthened according to your day. He is nearest, when He seems furthest away. I heard from Keble a day or two since, and he wished me to tell you they were thinking of you at Hursley. This is a day especially sacred to peace – the day of the Eternal Trinity, who were all blessed from eternity in themselves, and in the thought of whom the mind sees the end of its labours, the end of its birth, temptations, struggles, and sacrifices, its daily dyings and resurrections.

Pusey wrote to Keble on 5 June: 'God has been very merciful to me in this dispensation, and carried me on, step

23

by step, in a way I dared not hope. He sent Newman to me (whom I saw at my mother's wish against my inclination) in the first hour of sorrow; and it was like the visit of an angel.'

He wrote to Newman on 16 July: 'God bless and reward you for all your love and tender kindness towards us; I received day by day my share of it, with little acknowledgement, for words fail one, and one is stopped by a sort of αἰδώς ['reverent humility'] from thanking to the face for great kindness. Your first visit, "in the' embittered spirit's strife" was to me like that of an Angel sent from God: I shrunk from it beforehand, or from seeing any human face, and so I trust I may the more hope that it was God's doing. It seems as though it had changed, in a degree, the character of my subsequent life; and since it was quite unexpected and without any agency of my own. I hope it is His will that it should be so, and that He will keep me in the way, in which, as I hope, He brought me. God requite you for it all. It is a selfish wish to wish that one's prayers were better than they are: yet I hope that He will hear them, not according to their and my imperfection, but according to the greatness of the reason which I have to offer them, and according to His great mercy. I pray that He may make you what, as you say, there are so few of, a "great saint".'

Newman wrote and preached these words on the day the news came of Maria Pusey's death

All God's providences, all God's dealings with us, all His judgments, mercies, warnings, deliverances, tend to peace and repose as their ultimate issue. All our troubles and pleasures here, all our anxieties, fears, doubts, difficulties, hopes, encouragements, afflictions, losses, attainments, tend this one way. After Christmas, Easter, and Whitsuntide, comes Trinity Sunday, and the weeks that follow; and in like manner, after our soul's anxious travail; after the birth of the Spirit; after trial and temptation; after sorrow and pain; after daily dyings to the world; after daily risings unto holiness; at length comes that 'rest which remaineth unto the people of God.' After the fever of life; after wearinesses and sicknesses; fightings and despondings; languor and fretfulness; struggling and failing, struggling and succeeding; after all the changes and chances of this troubled unhealthy state, at length comes death, at length the White Throne of God, at length the Beatific Vision. After restlessness comes rest, peace, joy; – our eternal portion, if we be worthy; – the sight of the Blessed Three, the Holy One; the Three that bear witness in heaven; in light unapproachable; in glory without spot or blemish; in power without 'variableness, or shadow of turning.'

Henry Edward Manning's wife, Caroline was
desperately ill, and was to die on 24 July

14 July, 1837

My dear Manning,

You and yours have been much in my thoughts lately, and I have been continually doing that which you ask of me. It has truly grieved me to hear of the severe trial you are under, though really such trials are our portion. I think one may say it without exaggeration, but they who seek God do (as it were) come for afflictions. It is the way He shews His love, and to keep from so doing is His exception. I suppose we may consider His words to the Sons of Zebedee addressed to us. It often strikes me so when I am partaking the Holy Communion that I am but drinking in (perchance) temporal sorrow, according to His usual Providence. Hence St. Peter tells us not to think affliction a strange thing. Let this then, my dear Manning, be your comfort, – You are called to trouble as we all are, and the severer the more God loves you. He may mercifully consider your present distress and suspense sufficient for His inscrutable purposes – if so it will come to an end with nothing more. But anyhow be sure He does not willingly afflict us, nor will put a single grain's weight more of suffering than it is meet and good for you to bear – and be sure too that with your suffering your support will grow, and that if in His great wisdom and love He take away the desire of your eyes, it will only be to bring her really nearer to you. For those we love are not nearest to us when in the flesh, but they come into our very hearts as being spiritual beings, when they are removed from us. Alas! it is hard to persuade

26

oneself this, when we have the presence and are without experience of the absence of those we love; yet the absence is often more than the presence, even were this all, that our treasure being removed hence, leads us to think more of Heaven and less of earth.

Newman preaches on 'Endurance, the Christian's Portion' which he wrote after sending the letter to Manning

To their surprise, as time goes on, they find that their lot is changed. They find that in one shape or other adversity happens to them. If they refuse to afflict themselves, God afflicts them. One blow falls, they are startled; it passes over, it is well; they expect nothing more. Another comes; they wonder; 'Why is this?' they ask; they think that the first should be their security against the second; they bear it, however; and it passes too. Then a third comes; they almost murmur; they have not yet mastered the great doctrine that endurance is their portion. O simple soul, is it not the law of thy being to endure since thou camest to Christ? Why camest thou but to endure? Why didst thou taste His heavenly feast, but that it might work in thee? Why didst thou kneel beneath His hand, but that He might leave on thee the print of His wounds? Why wonder then that one sorrow does not buy off the next? Does one drop of rain absorb the second? Does the storm cease because it has begun? Understand thy place in God's kingdom, and rejoice, not complain, that in thy day thou hast thy lot with Prophets and Apostles. Envy not the gay and thriving world. Religious persons ask, 'Why are we so marked out for crosses? Others get on in the world; others are prosperous; their schemes turn out well, and their families settle happily; there is no anxiety, no bereavement among them, while the world fights against us.' This is what they sometimes say, though with some exaggeration certainly, for almost all men, sooner or later, have their troubles, and Christians, as well as others, have their spiritual comforts.

Samuel Wilberforce, Archdeacon of Winchester, lost his wife, Emily

12 March, 1841

My dear [Samuel] Wilberforce,

I have just heard from Henry the dreadful blow with which it has pleased a good Providence to visit you – and I hope you will not think a line or two intrusion merely to say that I very much wish to sympathise with you, though I know no one can – except indeed He who has sent you the affliction. Depend upon it, He does nothing in vain – and He will enable you to bear what He puts upon you. I speak what I from my heart feel when I say that I do think it shows that you are an object of His special care and love. He lets the world go on its course, and have every thing at its will. But He deals otherwise with you.

We must trust in God …

The Gospel of the day then sets before us the duty of *faith*, and rests it upon God's almightiness or omnipotence, as it is called. Nothing is too hard for Him, and we believe what the Church tells us of His deeds and providences, because He can do whatsoever He will. But there is another grace which the Gospel teaches us, and that is *hope* or *trust*. You observe that when the storm came, the disciples were in great *distress*. They thought some great calamity was coming on them. Therefore Christ said to them, 'Why are ye *fearful*?' Hope and fear are contrary to each other; they feared because they did not hope. To hope is not only to believe in God, but to believe and be certain that He loves us and means well to us; and therefore it is a great Christian grace. … He said to the disciples when the storm arose, 'Why are ye *fearful*?' That is, 'you ought to hope, you ought to trust, you ought to repose your heart on Me. I am not only almighty, but I am all-merciful. I have come on earth because I am most loving to you. Why am I here, why am I in human flesh, why have I these hands which I stretch out to you, why have I these eyes from which the tears of pity flow, except that I wish you well, that I wish to save you? The storm cannot hurt you if *I* am with you. Can you be better placed than under My protection? Do you doubt My power or My will, do you think Me *negligent* of you that I sleep in the ship, and *unable* to help except I am awake? Wherefore do you doubt? Wherefore do you fear? Have I been so long with you, and you do not yet trust Me and cannot remain in peace and quiet by My side?'

In this letter to the Duchess of Norfolk, he commiserates on the premature death of her husband (in November 1860). The new Duke, Henry, was only 14

13 March, 1861

My dear Duchess,

… I saw, a most happy home, happy in its own virtues, in its devotion and its good works, a home written doubtless in God's eternal book; and its sunshine has especially rested in my mind, because it so tenderly expressed its sympathy to me in a season of anxiety.

I think the memory of it will remain with me, while I live. And to you, when the first suffering is over, it will surely be an anticipation of heaven, till you are taken thither. What will be the joy, if we are worthy, to be admitted to the Holy Family above, who in their own persons have known the sorrows of separation, and who will then repair for us our broken ties, never again to be undone?

Give my love to Henry.

Love of home and family

We gain much for a time from fellowship with each other. It is a relief to us, as fresh air to the fainting, or meat and drink to the hungry, or a flood of tears to the heavy in mind. It is a soothing comfort to have those whom we may make our confidants; a comfort to have those to whom we may look for sympathy. Love of home and family in these and other ways is sufficient to make this life tolerable to the multitude of men, which otherwise it would not be; but still, after all, our affections exceed such exercise of them, and demand what is more stable. Do not all men die? are they not taken from us? are they not as uncertain as the grass of the field? ... Life passes, riches fly away, popularity is fickle, the senses decay, the world changes, friends die. One alone is constant; One alone is true to us; One alone can be true; One alone can be all things to us; One alone can supply our needs; One alone can train us up to our full perfection; One alone can give a meaning to our complex and intricate nature; One alone can give us tune and harmony; One alone can form and possess us.

Newman wrote to Henry Bowden as he also wrote to their children, on the death of his wife, Marianne

28 June, 1864

My dear Henry

We have been full of your great trial, and have said many Masses for your dear wife, and for you, and all your children. God has struck you most heavily but your dear children will rise up and console you. And God Himself, who has afflicted you, will be your best Comforter and Friend.

She is now in peace and rest – for her great and long sufferings have been her deliverance from what she might have had to suffer after death. For myself, thinking of her, *this* is the great consolation. I feel that I have a great loss myself, the loss of one so kind, so gentle, so open and true a friend, whom I sincerely admired and loved, who talked with me so frankly and familiarly, and made me know her by that most winning ease of her conversation, – ah! it is a great distress to think I shall not see her again, – but still to know that the worst is over, that all the terrible suspense of pain and dying is ended, that she has crossed the awful river, this is to me a thought full of comfort. She cannot die again – she has heaven before her – O what a thought of peace is this! And you too, my dear Henry, must feel it, and you will feel it more and more. I doubt not you will be supported through your suffering, and learn to love God more and more, the more He afflicts you.

Thank you for the kind thoughtfulness of your letter – Your dear girls will let me know how you are.

Cf. also p. 10–11

Let us labour to enter into our rest

O how great a good will it be, if, when this troublesome life is over, we in our turn also enter into that same rest, – if the time shall one day come, when we shall enter into His tabernacle above, and hide ourselves under the shadow of His wings; if we shall be in the number of those blessed dead who die in the Lord, and rest from their labour. Here we are tossing upon the sea, and the wind is contrary. All through the day we are tried and tempted in various ways. We cannot think, speak, or act, but infirmity and sin are at hand. But in the unseen world, where Christ has entered, all is peace. There is the eternal Throne, and a rainbow round about it, like unto an emerald; and in the midst of the throne the Lamb that has been slain, and has redeemed many people by His blood: and round about the throne four and twenty seats for as many elders, all clothed in white raiment, and crowns of gold upon their heads. And four living beings full of eyes before and behind. And seven Angels standing before God, and doing His pleasure unto the ends of the earth. And the Seraphim above. And withal, a great multitude which no man can number, of all nations, and kindreds, and people, and tongues, clothed with white robes, and palms in their hands. 'These are they which came out of great tribulation, and have washed their robes and made them white in the blood of the Lamb.'[1] 'They shall hunger no more, neither thirst any more; neither shall the sun light on them, nor any heat.' 'There is no more death, neither sorrow nor crying, neither any more pain; for the former things are passed away.'[2] Nor

[1] Rev 7, 14
[2] Rev 21, 4

any more sin; nor any more guilt; no more remorse; no more punishment; no more penitence; no more trial; no infirmity to depress us; no affection to mislead us; no passion to transport us; no prejudice to blind us; no sloth, no pride, no envy, no strife; but the light of God's countenance, and a pure river of water of life, clear as crystal, proceeding out of the Throne. That is our *home*; here we are but on pilgrimage, and Christ is calling us home. He calls us to His many mansions, which He has prepared. And the Spirit and the Bride call us too, and all things will be ready for us by the time of our coming. 'Seeing then that we have a great High Priest that has passed into the heavens, Jesus the Son of God, let us hold fast our profession;' seeing we have 'so great a cloud of witnesses, let us lay aside every weight;' 'let us labour to enter into our rest;' 'let us come boldly unto the Throne of Grace, that we may obtain mercy, and find grace to help in time of need.'[3]

[3] Heb 4, 11.14.16; 12, 1

*Sir John Simeon, whose sons were at the Oratory
School, died in Fribourg on 21 May*

30 May, 1870

My dear Lady Simeon

Our good God has visited you with a dreadful blow, and
has put upon you a very heavy burden – but He will enable
you to sustain both.

He never will forsake you or afflict you overmuch, He
will ever be with you – Already, I am sure, He has made you
feel how strong His strength is.

He has given you a brave spirit, and He will both try it
and reward it.

It is a most dear and pleasant thought, as to him whom
we have lost, to think how much he has gained by our losing
him – There is now an end with him of all distress, anxiety,
heaviness, perplexity, an end for ever.

No one can know as you know, how honest and true
were all his thoughts, and how beautiful his inward self. God
gave him many gifts. He gave him uprightness and reli-
giousness of mind – and amid severe trials, has led him
forward, and at length brought him through and out of this
scene of confusion and infirmity into that state of being
which is true and eternal. Shadows have departed for him,
and he is with his God. Those who have gone from us, have,
so far, a blessing which the best and holiest of men cannot
have here. He is beyond sin, trial, fear and uncertainty. If we
had the power of bringing him back by wishing, we could
not bring ourselves to wish it.

May we be worthy of God's goodness to us

Nay, even before the end comes, Christians, on looking back on years past, will feel, at least in a degree, that Christ has been with them, though they knew it not, only believed it, at the time. They will even recollect then the burning of their hearts. Nay, though they seemed not even to believe any thing at the time, yet afterwards, if they have come to Him in sincerity, they will experience a sort of heavenly fragrance and savour of immortality, when they least expect it, rising upon their minds, as if in token that God has been with them, and investing all that has taken place, which before seemed to them but earthly, with beams of glory. And this is true, in one sense, of all the rites and ordinances of the Church, of all providences that happen to us; that, on looking back on them, though they seemed without meaning at the time, elicited no strong feeling, or were even painful and distaste-ful, yet if we come to them and submit to them in faith, they are afterwards transfigured, and we feel that it has been good for us to be there; and we have a testimony, as a reward of our obedience, that Christ has fulfilled His promise, and, as He said, is here through the Spirit, though He be with the Father.

May He enable us to make full trial of His bounty, and to obtain a full measure of blessing. 'There is a river, the streams whereof shall make glad the city of God, the holy place of the tabernacles of the Most High. God is in the midst of her; she shall not be moved: God shall help her and that right early ... Be still, and know that I am God, I will be exalted among the heathen, I will be exalted in the earth. The Lord of hosts is with us; the God of Jacob is our refuge.'[1]

[1] Ps 46, 4.5.10.11

37

Hope-Scott's first wife, Charlotte, died on 26 October, leaving three small children

31 October, 1858

My dear Hope Scott

Fr Flanagan who is with me, and all our Fathers, have said, or will say, Mass for your intention.

I could not find words to use, when I wrote to you the other day, nor can I now.

God is so good in His heaviest visitations. You have one of the most enduring afflictions which *can* be – but it is the pledge of the most enduring mercies on you and yours. You will have one in heaven to watch over you all, with that peculiar affection, which can be hers alone.

Well may we say, God's will be done – for His will is so loving. You must know this; though I, who have lived longer, know it more.

He will support you, though no one else can. We, who love you, can but beg Him to do so – but that I do continually.

Newman concludes a sermon with a plea that God will guide us on our way even to our life's end

O Lord, support us all the day long until the shadows lengthen and the evening comes and the busy world is hushed and the fever of life is over, and our work is done. Then, Lord, in your mercy, grant us a safe lodging, a holy rest, and peace at the last.

Richard Pope had married, for the second time,
Elizabeth Phillips in 1867, but she died in 1874
leaving four children

13 March, 1874

My dear Richard Pope

Thank you for your affectionate note. It would be wonderful indeed, if we did not feel much for the loss of dear Bessie, both for our own sake, and then more especially for yours. We knew, much as we might love her, (and I assure you, though no one knew it, I never could look at her sweet bright face without great pleasure, and, I may say, joy,) we could not love her, much less miss her and mourn for her, as you had loved and you would mourn, and that made and makes us feel for you the more, for the very reason that we sorrow so much even on our own account ...

The Invisible World

And in that other world are the souls also of the dead. They too, when they depart hence, do not cease to exist, but they retire from this visible scene of things; or, in other words, they cease to act towards us and before us *through our senses,* they live as they lived before; but that outward frame, through which they were able to hold communion with other men, is in some way, we know not how, separated from them, and dries away and shrivels up as leaves may drop off a tree.

Lord Coleridge was still grieving for his wife who had died in February

28 December, 1878

My dear Lord Coleridge,

No one can relieve your bitter pain but He who has wounded you. Others can but look on, but pray Him to be merciful. And, though it is so difficult to realise it, and we use the words as words of course, still, it is true, that, specially, when He takes away the desire of our eyes with a stroke, He is then most merciful to us. The seemingly most cruel providences are the most loving.

What is the good of my saying this? It shows my impotence, but it is all that I can do ...

Suffering likens us to Christ

… but Almighty God, while He chose the latter [worldly trial] as the portion of His Saints, sanctified it by His heavenly grace, to be their great benefit. He rescues them from the selfishness of worldly comfort without surrendering them to the selfishness of worldly pain. He brings them into pain, that they may be like what Christ was, and may be led to think of Him, not of themselves. He brings them into trouble, that they may be near Him. When they mourn, they are more intimately in His presence than they are at any other time. Bodily pain, anxiety, bereavement, distress, are to them His forerunners. It is a solemn thing, while it is a privilege, to look upon those whom He thus visits. Why is it that men would look with fear and silence at the sight of the spirit of some friend departed, coming to them from the grave? Why would they abase themselves and listen awfully to any message he brought them? Because he would seem to come from the very presence of God. And in like manner, when a man, in whom dwells His grace, is lying on the bed of suffering, or when he has been stripped of his friends and is solitary, he has, in a peculiar way, tasted of the powers of the world to come, and exhorts and consoles with authority. He who has been long under the rod of God, becomes God's possession.

The Death of Children

Taken from the World to God

Newman wrote to console Archdeacon Froude on the death of his daughter, Phillis, and his son, Hurrell

11 August, 1836

My dear Sir,

This morning's paper gave me the sad intelligence of the affliction which it has pleased God to send to you and yours. I do not like to keep silence, though I almost fear intruding upon you by writing. May God in His mercy, as I doubt not He will, recompense all this tenfold to you in the world to come. Surely it must be intended for some very great good, for some very great joy hereafter – a joy which, on its coming, will abundantly overbalance the present suffering. Every one here, who is left in Oxford, feels it very much – and sympathizes with you deeply – indeed who would not? But I cannot doubt that He who thus visits, will support you all under it; of course He puts nothing upon us above our strength. Yet even I, who had seen her who is not taken away, merely as a stranger, saw quite enough to understand what a blow it must be. Really, quite independently of my feeling for all at Dartington, my heart quite aches from the thought of what excellence and sweetness is taken from the world in her removal.

The sympathy of Christ

Let us take to ourselves these comfortable thoughts, both in the contemplation of our own death, or upon the death of our friends. Wherever faith in Christ is, there is Christ himself. He said to Martha 'Believest thou this?' Wherever there is a heart to answer, 'Lord, I believe', there Christ is present. There our Lord vouchsafes to stand, though unseen – whether over the bed of death or over the grave; whether we ourselves are sinking or those who are dear to us. Blessed be his name! nothing can rob us of this consolation: we will be as certain, through his grace, that he is standing over us in love, as though we saw him.

Henry Wilberforce had informed Newman of the death of his daughter, Florence, aged four

24 October, 1841

My dearest Henry,

Your note took me by surprise, and I have thought much of you and your wife. I know how severe a blow it must be yet what a comfort too! Is it not a comfort to have given a child to God? Is it not the best kind of dedication? What could you desire more? If she had lived to old age, would it not be that she might die, and (as your hope would be) *that* she might die to *God*! See there you have your prayers fulfilled to you, and that before your eyes. You have not the event left in uncertainty, but God has granted to you an assurance which cannot be given when children grow up and die. Alas! in the present state of Christendom is it not a special comfort to know one tenth which none will dispute, and that no other than the eternal salvation of a soul dear to us? You may say that she is blessed for ever, and there is none to gainsay you.

The joy of heaven

Shine forth, O Lord, as when on Thy Nativity Thine Angels visited the shepherds; let Thy glory blossom forth as bloom and foliage on the trees; change with Thy mighty power this visible world into that diviner world, which as yet we see not; destroy what we see, that it may pass and be transformed into what we believe. Bright as the sun, and the sky, and the clouds; green as are the leaves and the fields; sweet as is the singing of the birds; we know that they are not all, and we will not take up with a part for the whole. They proceed from a centre of love and goodness, which is God himself; but they are not His fulness; they speak of heaven, but they are not heaven; they are but as stray beams and dim reflections of His Image; they are but crumbs from the table. We are looking for the coming of the day of God, when all this outward world, fair though it be, shall perish; when the heavens shall be burnt, and the earth melt away. We can bear the loss, for we know it will be but the removing of a veil. We know that what we see is as a screen hiding from us God and Christ, and His Saints and Angels. And we earnestly desire and pray for the dissolution of all that we see, from our longing after that which we do not see.

O blessed they indeed, who are destined for the sight of those wonders in which they now stand, at which they now look, but which they do not recognize! Blessed they who shall at length behold what as yet mortal eye hath not seen and faith only enjoys! Those wonderful things of the new world are even now as they shall be then. They are immortal and eternal; and the soul who shall then be made conscious of them, will see them in their calmness and their majesty where they ever have been ... When we find ourselves after long rest gifted with fresh powers, vigorous with the seed of eternal life within us, able to love God as we wish, conscious that all trouble, sorrow, pain, anxiety, bereavement, is over for ever, blessed in the full affection of those earthly friends whom we loved so poorly, and could protect so feebly, while they were with us in the flesh, and above all, visited by the immediate visible ineffable Presence of God Almighty, with his Only-begotten Son our Lord Jesus Christ, and His Co-equal Spirit, that great sight in which is the fulness of joy and pleasure for evermore – what deep, incommunicable, unimaginable thoughts will be then upon us! what depths will be stirred up within us! what secret harmonies awakened, of which human nature seemed incapable! Earthly words are indeed all worthless to minister to such high anticipations. Let us close our eyes and keep silence.

Newman wrote to Pusey on hearing that his daughter Lucy, aged fourteen was desperately ill (she died three days later)

19 April, 1844

My dear Pusey,

You may fancy what an heart ache your note of to-day has given me. Yet all is well, as you know better than I can say. What would you more than is granted you as regards dear Lucy? She was given to you to be made an heir of Heaven. Have you not been allowed to perform that part towards her? You have done your work – what remains but to present it finished to Him who put it upon you? You are presenting it to Him, you are allowed to do so, in the way most acceptable to Him, as a holy blameless sacrifice, not a sacrifice which the world has sullied, but as if a baptismal offering, perfected by long though kind and gentle sufferings. How fitly do her so touching words which you report to me accord with such thoughts as these! 'Love', which she asks for, is of course the grace which will complete the whole. Do you not bear in mind the opinion of theologians that it is the grace which supplies all things, supersedes all things, and is all in all? I believe they hold, though a dying person were in a desert, without any one at hand, love would be to him every thing. He has in it forgiveness of sins, communion of saints, and the presence of Christ. Dear Lucy has been made His in Baptism, she has been made His in suffering; and now she asks to be made His by love.

On the sympathy shown by God the Father

There is no one who has loved the world so well, as He who made it. None has so understood the human heart, and human nature, and human society in its diversified forms, none has so tenderly entered into and measured the greatness and the littleness of man, his doings and sufferings, his circumstances and his fortunes, none has felt such profound compassion for his ignorance and guilt, his present rebellion and his prospects hereafter, as the Omniscient. What He has actually done for us is the proof of this. 'God so loved the world, as to give His Only-begotten Son.'[1]

[1] John 3, 16

Lady Lothian's son, John, died at Ushaw College aged fourteen

26 January, 1855

To the Marchioness of Lothian

I have heard that dear John has been thought too good for this world by Him who so lovingly brought Him near Himself a year ago.[1] Ever since I heard of his illness I have been thinking of him. I saw him last year at Ushaw, and was so struck by him that I talked of him to others for some time after. He came into my room of his own accord, and made friends with me in an instant. For him, how can I but rejoice that he should be taken out of this dark world in the freshness and bloom of his innocence and piety. But it comes over me most keenly that if once seeing him made me love him so much, what must it have been to you? And oh! how sad in a human light that you and his sisters should have been so far away – and poor Ralph in bed[2] and unable to go to him!

[1] He had become a Catholic in 1854
[2] Lord Ralph Kerr his brother was ill with pleurisy at the Birmingham Oratory

The God who gives joy to our youth

Blessed are they who give the flower of their days, and their strength of soul and body to Him; blessed are they who in their youth turn to Him who gave His life for them, and would fain give it to them and implant it in them, that they may live forever. Blessed are they who resolve – come good, come evil, come sunshine, come tempest, come honour, come dishonour – that He shall be their Lord and Master, their King and God! They will come to a perfect end, and to peace at the last.

Phillipps' son Everard died aged twenty-two in Delhi, three days after being awarded the Victoria Cross

24 November, 1857

My dear Mr Phillipps

This requires no answer. It is merely to tell you that I have been this morning saying Mass for the repose of the soul of your dear son. Nothing, I know well, that others can say, can enable you and Mrs Phillipps to support such a blow. It is the consolation which comes from above, and that alone, which can aid you – and that you have abundantly. And as time goes on, the pain will be less and less, and the light of divine consolation will become brighter and brighter – for you will understand, more than anyone else, how great a thing it is to have a son, secured from the ten thousand temptations of the world, and safely lodged in unchangeable blessedness.

Meanwhile, be sure you have the deep sympathy of all who know and love you, and their best prayers.

We go into the presence of Christ

There is a peculiar feeling with which we regard the dead. What does this arise from? – that he is absent? No; for we do not feel the same towards one who is merely distant, though he be at the other end of the earth. Is it because in this life we shall never see him again? No, surely not; because we may be perfectly certain we shall never see him when he goes abroad, we may know he is to die abroad, and perhaps he does die abroad; but will any one say that, when the news of his death comes, our feeling when we think of him is not quite changed? Surely it is the passing into another state which impresses itself upon us, and makes us speak of him as we do, – I mean, with a sort of awe. We cannot tell what he is now, – what his relations to us, – what he knows of us. We do not understand him, – we do not see him. He is passed into the land 'that is very far off;' but it is not at all certain that he has not some mysterious hold over us. Thus his not being seen with our bodily eyes, while perchance he is present, makes the thought of him more awful. Apply this to the subject before us, and you will perceive that there is a sense, and a true sense, in which the *invisible* presence of God is more awful and overpowering than if we saw it. And so again, the presence of Christ, now that it is invisible, brings with it a host of high and mysterious feelings, such as nothing else can inspire. The thought of our Saviour, absent yet present, is like that of a friend taken from us, but, as it were, in dream returned to us, though in this case not in dream, but in reality and truth.

*Sir W.H. Archer, a long standing admirer, wrote
from Melbourne about the death of his son*

16 June, 1873

My dear Sir

... By the time this reaches you I trust time itself has done
much to soothe you, and has enabled you through the
clouds to see the Hand of Mercy afflicting you from special
love to you. I had a dear friend who has lately died. He lost
his only son – then, some years after a son was born to him,
and he lost him too – and then a third time, when a son
was born, he lost his wife at once, and now has died himself
leaving the wished-for child an orphan of only two years
old.[1] Some special good comes, I believe, from these severe
bereavements. They are the corresponding trials now to that
singular trial in the early times of giving up father and
mother, home and children for our Lord's sake.[2]

And God has tempered the blow by making all your
memories of the dear one you have lost, so pleasant because
so holy.

[1] Hope-Scott *cf.* p. 13f
[2] Matt 19, 29

In all suffering we can see the hand of God

By humbling ourselves now, we hope to escape humiliation then. By owning our faults now, we hope to avert the disclosures of that day. By judging our faults now, we hope to be spared that judgment which mercy tempers not. We prepare now to meet our God; we retire, as it were, to our sick room, and put our house in order. We 'remember our Creator in the days of our youth' and strength 'while the evil days come not, nor the years draw nigh, in which is no pleasure'; ere 'the keepers of the house tremble, and the strong men bow themselves, and the doors are shut in the streets, and the daughters of music are brought low, and desire fails: or ever the silver cord be loosed, or the golden bowl be broken, or the pitcher be broken at the fountain, or the wheel broken at the cistern.'[1] We leave the goods of earth before they leave us.

Let us not shrink from this necessary work; let us not suffer indolence or carnal habits to get the better of us. Let us not yield to disgust or impatience; let us not fear as we enter into the cloud. Let us recollect that it is *His* cloud that overshadows us. It is no earthly sorrow or pain, such as worketh death; but it is a bright cloud of godly sorrow, 'working repentance to salvation not to be repented of'.[2] It is the hand of God which is upon us; 'let us humble ourselves therefore under the mighty hand of God, that He may exalt us in due time'.[3]

[1] Eccles 12, 1.3.4.6
[2] 2 Cor 7, 10
[3] I Pet 5, 6

The Loss of Friends

Those I Have Loved Long Since and Lost Awhile

Newman preached the funeral sermon for Walter Mayers, who was the 'human means' of his religious conversion in Autumn 1816 at the school in Ealing where Mayers was then a master

We loved him in the Lord, we were knit together unto him in the Lord – the Lord that brought both him and us, has joined together all his Saints in a mystical body – who can ever separate us from Him and from each other?

Our confidence is in God

Thus the true Christian pierces through the veil of this world and sees the next. He holds intercourse with it; he addresses God, as a child might address his parent, with as clear a view of Him, and with as unmixed a confidence in Him; with deep reverence indeed, and godly fear and awe, but still with certainty and exactness: as St. Paul says, 'I know whom I have believed',[1] with the prospect of judgment to come to sober him, and the assurance of present grace to cheer him.

[1] 2 Tim 1, 12

Newman did not expect J.W. Bowden to live but preached that one must not give up hope

Take up thy portion, then, Christian soul, and weigh it well, and learn to love it. Thou wilt find, if thou art Christ's, in spite of what the world fancies, that after all, even at this day, endurance, in a special sense, *is* the lot of those who offer themselves to be servants of the King of sorrows ... They are soldiers in Christ's army; they fight against 'things that are seen,' and they have 'all these things against them.' To their surprise, as time goes on, they find that their lot is changed. They find that in one shape or other adversity happens to them. If they refuse to afflict themselves, God afflicts them. One blow falls, they are startled; it passes over, it is well; they expect nothing more. Another comes; they wonder; 'Why is this?' they ask; they think that the first should be their security against the second; they bear it, however; and it passes too. Then a third comes; they almost murmur; they have not yet mastered the great doctrine that endurance is their portion.

Never while the Church lasts, will the words of old Jacob be reversed – all things here are against us but God; but if God be for us, who can really be against us? If He is in the midst of us, how shall we be moved? If Christ has died and risen again, what death can come upon us, though we be made to die daily? what sorrow, pain, humiliation, trial, but must end as His has ended, in a continual resurrection into His new world, and in a nearer and nearer approach to Him? He pronounced a blessing over His Apostles, and they have scattered it far and wide all over the earth unto this day. It runs as follows: 'Peace I leave with you, My peace I give unto you; not as the world giveth, give I unto you.' 'These things I have spoken unto you, that in Me ye might have peace. In the world ye shall have tribulation; but be of good cheer, I have overcome the world.'[1]

[1] John 14, 27; 16, 33

Newman later writes to his friend Ambrose St John

16 September, 1844

My dear St John,

... I am full of wrong and miserable feelings, which it is useless to detail – so grudging and sullen when I should be thankful. Of course when one sees so blessed an end and that at the termination of so blameless a life, of one who really fed on our ordinances and got strength from them – and see the same continued in a whole family, the little children finding quite a solace of their pain in the Daily Prayer, it is impossible not to feel more at ease in our Church, at least a sort of Zoar,[1] a place of refuge and temporary rest because of the sternness of the way. Only may we be kept from unlawful security, lest we have Moab and Ammon[2] for our progeny, the enemies of Israel.

After Bowden's death, Newman noted 'to think
that he left me still dark as to what the way of
truth was, and what I ought to do ...'

17 September, 1844
My dear Keble,

As you saw, I was writing my note, and the unexpected
news came. I did not know when it had taken place and I
left home, at Mrs B[owden]'s wish, not knowing where I
was going ...

He died, and he lies, in a room I have known these 24
years – the principal drawing room – so many persons have
I seen there, so kind to me – they are all gone. The furni-
ture is all the same – the ornaments on the mantlepiece –
and there lies now my oldest friend, so dear to me – and I
with so little of faith or hope, as dead as a stone, and detest-
ing myself.

Newman also wrote to his sister Harriet

19 September, 1844

Jemima will tell you some things about dear Bowden. His end was as peaceful and beautiful as became such a blameless life; so cheerful, so playful, so tender, smiling through his tears, and in nothing great or small wishing any thing whatever but what supreme Love and Wisdom thought best for him. Leaving all he loved, securely in the hands of Him who could supply all his loss, and only afraid that he felt too little dread of his summons to another world.

[1] Gen 19, 20–24
[2] Judg, 3, 13

Our journey to the God who made us

But let us follow the course of a soul thus casting off the world, and cast off by it. It goes forth as a stranger on a journey. Man seems to die and to be no more, when he is but quitting us, and is really beginning to live. Then he sees sights which before it did not even enter into his mind to conceive, and the world is even less to him than he to the world. Just now he was lying on the bed of sickness, but in that moment of death what an awful change has come over him! What a crisis for him! There is stillness in the room that lately held him; nothing is doing there, for he is gone, he now belongs to others; he now belongs entirely to the Lord who bought him; to Him he returns.

Lead Kindly Light

Help Thou my Darkness, Lord, till I am Light

Newman commiserates with Bowden's wife

25 September, 1844

My dear Mrs Bowden,

... I do not know how to touch upon the subject nearest my heart now in a letter – yet before I began, I intended to have said several things, which it is so abrupt, when it comes to the point, to set down in writing. It is impossible you should know the feeling which John raised in the minds of persons who knew him ever so little towards himself and towards all of you, or the sorrow which his loss now causes. I know one person years ago whom the sight of him in his family hindered being able to say that celibacy was more excellent in its nature than married life – i.e. was just the thing which touched and moved him – and the other day some one was saying that to see him with those who were dear to him around him just realized the idea one had of a holy family. And these are but the expression of a very wide spread feeling – which I mention for the very reason that it is so seldom expressed in words, and cannot be put into words on the moment, and because I was so little able the other day to show you anything such as you wished in letters I had received.

On the death of St. Joseph

For thirty years He lived with Mary and Joseph and thus formed a shadow of the Heavenly Trinity on earth. O the perfection of that sympathy which existed between the three! ... The first weakening of that unison was when Joseph died. It was no jar in the sound, for to the last moment of his life, he was one with them, and the sympathy between the three became more intense, and more sweet, while it was brought into new circumstances and had a wider range in the months of his declining, his sickness, and death. Then it was like an air ranging through a number of notes performed perfectly and exactly in time and tune by all three. But it ended in a lower note than before, and when Joseph went, a weaker one. Not that Joseph, though so saintly, added much in volume of sound to the other two, but sympathy, by its very meaning, implies number, and, on his death, one, out of the three harps, was unstrung and silent. O what a moment of sympathy between the three, the moment before Joseph died – they supporting and hanging over him, he looking at them and reposing in them with undivided, unreserved, supreme, devotion, for he was in the arms of God and the Mother of God. As a flame shoots up and expires, so was the ecstasy of that last moment ineffable, for each knew and thought of the reverse which was to follow on the snapping of that bond.

Elizabeth Lenthall had been Newman's helper in
St Mary's. She was well known to his sister

2 December, 1841

My dear Jemima,

... It is about poor Miss Lenthall, who is visited by an
internal cancer, which is not only quite incapable of cure,
but from its position cannot be treated or relieved – and
which opiates will only make worse in other ways. Except
that God holds the terms of pain and refreshment in His
own hand, and can compensate as He will, one should say,
humanly speaking the more speedily the disease runs its
course the better. Is not this most sad and painful to hear?
Ogle[1] gave me quite a fearful account of it. Yet He who
made the pains of Martyrs pleasant, can make her bear this.
She knows that the case is hopeless, and has already felt the
pains of it, which must increase; but she does not know the
name.

[1] James Adey Ogle, Aldrich Professor of Medicine

All suffering has an end

Yet how different must the state of the Church appear to beings who can contemplate it as a whole, who have contemplated it for ages, – as the Angels! We know what experience does for us in this world. Men get to see and understand the course of things, and by what rules it proceeds; and they can foretell what will happen, and they are not surprised at what does happen. They take the history of things as a matter of course. They are not startled that things happen in one way, not in another; it is the rule. Night comes after day; winter after summer; cold, frost and snow, in their season. Certain illnesses have their times of recurrence, or visit at certain ages. All things go through a process, – they have a beginning and an end. Grown men know this, but it is otherwise with children. To them every thing that they see is strange and surprising. They by turns feel wonder, admiration, or fear at every thing that happens; they do not know whether it will happen again or not; and they know nothing of the regular operation of causes, or the connexion of those effects which result from one and the same cause. And so too as regards the state of our souls under the Covenant of mercy; the heavenly hosts, who see what is going on upon earth, well understand, even from having seen it often, what is the course of a soul travelling from hell to heaven. They have seen, again and again, in number-less instances, that suffering is the path to peace; that they that sow in tears shall reap in joy; and that what was true of Christ is fulfilled in a measure in His followers.

This memoir was written by Newman about Fr Joseph Gordon, one of the early members of the Oratory, to whom he dedicated 'The Dream of Gerontius'

He languished and sank; got worse and worse; and at the end of nearly three months, on 13th February 1853, he died at Bath. He is in the arms of his God. We all loved him with a deep affection; we lamented him with all our hearts; we keenly feel his loss to this day. But the Father's[1] bereavement is of a special kind, and his sorrow is ever new.

We are warned by the Apostle 'not to be sorrowful as others who have not hope'.[2] For dear Father Joseph the change is gain; nor to us, in spite of the appearance of things, is it really loss. He who takes away can compensate; and our Holy Father, St Philip, himself reminds us that 'God has no need of men'. His mercies abound and continue. Every year brings with it fresh instances of them. In our *degree*, we may humbly use the same Apostle's words, and bless 'the Father of mercies and the God of all comfort, who comforteth us in all our tribulation; for, as the sufferings of Christ abound in us, so also by Christ doth our comfort abound'.[3]

---

[1] The Father is the title given to the Provost, the Superior of the Oratory, i.e. Newman himself
[2] I Thess 4, 13
[3] 2 Cor 1, 3–5

This is what shall be in the end without end

Without Thee eternity would be another name for eternal misery. In Thee alone have I that which can stay me up for ever: Thou alone art the food of my soul. Thou alone art inexhaustible, and ever offerest to me something new to know, something new to love. At the end of millions of years, I shall know Thee so little, that I shall seem to myself only beginning. At the end of millions of years I shall find in Thee the same, or rather, greater sweetness than at first, and shall seem then only to be beginning to enjoy Thee; and so on for eternity I shall ever be a little child beginning to be taught the rudiments of Thy infinite Divine nature. For Thou art Thyself the seat and centre of all good, and the only substance in this universe of shadows, and the heaven in which blessed spirits live and rejoice.

Newman writes to Hope-Scott about a fellow lawyer, Edward Badeley, who had helped him during the Achilli trial and had just died

31 March, 1868

My dear Hope Scott

What a heavy, sudden, unexpected blow – I shall not see him now, till I cross the stream which he has crossed. How dense is our ignorance of the future, a darkness which can be felt, and the keenest consequence and token of the Fall. Till we remind ourselves of what we are, – in a state of punishment, – such surprises make us impatient, and almost angry, alas!

But my blow is nothing to yours, though you had the great consolation of sitting by his side and being with him to the last. What a fulness of affection he poured out on you and yours – and how he must have rejoiced to have your faithful presence with him, while he was going. This is your joy and your pain.

Now he has the recompense for that steady, well-ordered, perpetual course of devotion and obedience, which I ever admired in him, and felt to be so much above any thing that I could reach. All or most of us have said Mass for him, I am sure, this morning; certainly we two have who are here.

Christ is with us in the 'warfare of life'

Christ has gone before, – Christ has given us an example,
that we may follow His steps. He went through far more,
infinitely more, than we can be called to suffer. Our
brethren have gone through much more; and they seem to
encourage us by their success, and to sympathize in our
essay. Now it is our turn; and all ministering spirits keep
silence and look on. O let not your foot slip, or your eye be
false or your ear dull, or your attention flagging! Be not
dispirited; be not afraid; keep a good heart; be bold; draw
not back; – you will be carried through. Whatever troubles
come on you, of mind, body, or estate; from within or from
without; from chance or from intent; from friends or foes;
– whatever your trouble be, though you be lonely, O children of a heavenly Father, be not afraid! quit you like men
in your day; and when it is over, Christ will receive you to
Himself, and your heart shall rejoice, and your joy no man
taketh from you.

Christ is already in that place of peace, which is all in all.
He is on the right hand of God. He is hidden in the bright-
ness of the radiance which issues from the everlasting
Throne. He is in the very abyss of peace, where there is no
voice of tumult or distress, but a deep stillness, – stillness,
that greatest and most awful of all goods which we can
fancy, – that most perfect of joys, the utter, profound, ineffable tranquillity of the Divine Essence. He has entered into
His rest.

Fr. Ambrose St John died on 28 April. He had been Newman's most devoted colleague for over thirty years

9 May, 1875

My dear Mrs Wilberforce,

... I can only say, 'Lord, he whom Thou lovest, is sick',[1] and leave the event to Him. I seem as if grief would kill me – but I cannot get beyond leaving the event to God. He knows what I wish, but why should I make any petition, when He knows what is good for us all? ...

[1] John 11, 3

That final leaving of the world, we call death

Why are people unwilling to die? What is the one reason? There is no pain in it. Because they leave what is known; they go to what is unknown. They leave the sun, etc., they leave their families, their schemes, their wealth.

Oh, how much is implied in this! Men witness against themselves. They are afraid to leave this life; they own they are going to the unknown, yet they are unwilling to make that unknown known. Do lay this to heart; you are going to the unknown.

Now I will tell you what you are going to – not to creatures as here, but to God.

God alone is our eternal happiness

Before that [the resurrection of the dead], the departed, as
such, are not members of the heavenly 'Curia'. Not till then,
if even then: – our duty being, when we lose those who had
been hitherto the light of our eyes, not so much to look
forward to meeting them again, as to take their removal as
an occasion to fix our thoughts more steadily, and our love,
on Him who is the true lover of souls, recollecting the great
danger we lie under of making an idol of the creature,
instead of cherishing the intimate conviction that God
alone can be our peace, joy, and blessedness.

About the death of Fr. St John

19 June, 1875

My dear Miss Geoghagan

... I can quite understand how a little child twines round the hearts of parents from its innocent sweetness and helplessness – and that the more, because, in the account I gave some friends of the illness of the friend I have lost, I recognized in him just those same looks which made me say to them that his face had on it a child's expression, so tender, gentle, and imploring. Thus both young and old, go 'as little children'[1] into the presence of their God ...

[1] Matt 18, 3

Eternal light shall shine upon them

If ever, through Thy grace, I attain to see Thee in heaven, I shall see nothing else but Thee, because I shall see all whom I see in Thee, and seeing them I shall see Thee. As I cannot see things here below, without light, and to see them is to see the rays which come from them, so in that eternal City, *Claritas Dei illuminavit eam, et lucerna ejus est Agnus* ('for the glory of God is its light, and its lamp is the Lamb' – Rev 21, 23)

Newman writes to his nephew on the death of his mother, and Newman's sister, Jemima

26 February, 1880

My very dear John,

Looking beyond this life, my first prayer, aim, and hope is that I may see God. The thought of being blest with the sight of earthly friends pales before that thought. I believe that I shall never die; this awful prospect would crush me, were it not that I trusted and prayed that it would be an eternity in God's presence. How is eternity a boon, unless He goes with it?

And for others dear to me, my one prayer is that they may see God.

It is the thought of God, His Presence, His strength which makes up, which repairs all bereavements.

> 'Give what Thou wilt, without Thee we are poor,
> And with Thee rich, take what Thou wilt away'

I prayed that it might be so, when I lost so many friends thirty-five years ago; what else could I look to?

On the subject of providence

But He has been more merciful than this – the hairs of our head numbered. Particular Providence everywhere and always. How was He to show this particular providence? By suspending the laws [of Nature] by miracles.

This He did. But that particular providence He has mercifully brought [out] in a distinct form, first in the Mosaic, and then in the Gospel economy. He has suspended His laws.

Especially when, after suffering, He ascended to heaven.

He promises us heaven. He has gone to prepare a place for us individually there ...

We think of meeting our *friends* in heaven; we do not think of Him who is the best of all friends.

Newman bids his friend Henry Wilberforce farewell

At the end of the Mass, Father Bertrand [Arthur Wilberforce] said something to Dr. Newman, and after a little whispering, the venerable man was conducted to the pulpit. For some minutes, however, he was utterly incapable of speaking, and stood, his face covered with his hands, making vain efforts to master his emotion. I was quite afraid he would have to give it up. At last, however, after two or three attempts, he managed to steady his voice and to tell us 'that he knew him so intimately [Henry Wilberforce] and loved him so much that it was almost impossible for him to command himself sufficiently to do what he had so unexpectedly been asked to do – viz., to bid his dear friend farewell. He had known him for fifty years, and though no doubt there were some there who knew his goodness better than he did, yet it seemed to him that no one could mourn him more than he did.' Then he drew a little outline of his life – of the position of comfort, and all 'that this world calls good,' in which he found himself, and of the prospects of advancement, 'if he had been an ambitious man'. 'When the word of the Lord came to him as it did to Abraham of old, to go forth from that pleasant home and from his friends, and all he held dear, and to become –' here he fairly broke down again, but, at last, lifting up his head again, finished his sentence – 'a fool for Christ's sake,' then he said that he now committed him to the hands of his Saviour.

Almighty God

Our Beginning and our Ending

Newman writes to Sr Gabriel du Boulay who had been seriously ill

29 December, 1876

My dear Child

How wonderful are God's ways, but how loving too, as we know well, He is all of them. You He had raised up again when we thought you were on the point of going to Him, and our dear Father Caswall who seemed so strong and well, is suddenly cast down and to all appearance is fast going.[1]

Only may we all go into His rest and peace, who is our centre and all-in-all, our beginning and our ending.

[1] Fr Caswall recovered but died in 1878, aged sixty-four

The beatific vision

We enter into our rest, by entering in with Him who, having wrought and suffered, has opened the kingdom of heaven to all believers. For half a year we stand still, as if occupied solely in adoring Him, and, with the Seraphim in the text, crying, 'Holy, Holy, Holy,' continually. All God's providences, all God's dealings with us, all His judgments, mercies, warnings, deliverances, tend to peace and repose as their ultimate issue. All our troubles and pleasures here, all our anxieties, fears, doubts, difficulties, hopes, encouragements, afflictions, losses, attainments, tend this one way. After Christmas, Easter, and Whitsuntide, comes Trinity Sunday, and the weeks that follow; and in like manner, after our soul's anxious travail; after the birth of the Spirit; after trial and temptation; after sorrow and pain; after daily dyings to the world; after daily risings unto holiness; at length comes that 'rest which remaineth unto the people of God.'[1] After the fever of life; after weariness and sicknesses; fightings and despondings; languor and fretfulness; struggling and failing, struggling and succeeding; after all the changes and chances of this troubled unhealthy state, at length comes death, at length the White Throne of God, at length the Beatific Vision. After restlessness comes rest, peace, joy; – our eternal portion, if we be worthy; – the sight of the Blessed Three, the Holy One; the Three that bear witness in heaven; in light unapproachable; in glory without spot or blemish; in power without 'variableness, or shadow of turning.' The Father God, the Son God, and the Holy Ghost God; the Father Lord, the Son Lord, and the Holy Ghost Lord; the

[1] Heb 4, 9

92

Father uncreate, the Son uncreate, and the Holy Ghost uncreate; the Father incomprehensible, the Son incomprehensible, and the Holy Ghost incomprehensible. For there is one Person of the Father, another of the Son, and another of the Holy Ghost; and such as the Father is, such is the Son, and such is the Holy Ghost; and yet there are not three Gods, nor three Lords, nor three incomprehensibles, nor three uncreated; but one God, one Lord, one uncreated, and one incomprehensible.

Newman writes to Fr. Vincent Hornyold about his brother in law Hubert Hibbert, an old boy of the Oratory School, who had just died

6 April, 1879

My dear Vincent

We were very much shocked and grieved to hear of dear Hubert's death. What you say of his affection for this place and for me is most pleasant to me and touches me much. Assure your sister how deeply I feel for her. But all God's Providences are good. Those which we now call most cruel, one day will seem to us most loving. How we then shall rejoice at those things which now are so overwhelming in their acute pain! Now we need great aids from Him to bear the present pain – and He will give those aids, sufficient, abundant, and more than abundant, more than equal to the suffering, to your Sister.

I will, please God, say three Masses for his dear soul. Ah, how strange it is that the young should be taken and the old left – but God knows what is best for all of us.

This is Newman's own prayer for a happy death

Oh, my Lord and Saviour, support me in that hour in the strong arms of thy sacraments, and by the fresh fragrance of thy consolations. Let the absolving words be said over me, and the holy oil sign and seal me, and thy own Body be my food, and thy Blood my sprinkling; and let my sweet Mother, Mary, breathe on me, and my angel whisper peace to me, and my glorious saints ... smile upon me; that in them all, and through them all, I may receive the gift of perseverance, and die, as I desire to live, in thy faith, in thy Church, in thy service, and in thy love. Amen.

The angels who ministered to Christ behold the face of God in heaven

Father, whose goodness none can know, but they
Who see Thee face to face,
By man hath come the infinite display
Of Thy victorious grace;
But fallen man – the creature of a day –
Skills not that love to trace.
It needs, to tell the triumph Thou hast wrought,
An Angel's deathless fire, an Angel's reach of thought.

It needs that very Angel, who with awe,
Amid the garden shade,
The great Creator in His sickness saw,
Soothed by a creature's aid,
And agonized, as victim of the Law
Which He Himself had made;
For who can praise Him in his depth and height,
But he who saw Him reel amid that solitary fight?

References